His tears in ink

By

Fred D. Warren

Table of Contents

Dedications

Preface

About the Author

Poem Listing:

Disclaimer Document

<u>Dedications</u>

A dedication to you, the reader

No matter how hard life gets do not throw in the towel. The road to success will not be easy, but if you keep fighting and pushing along the journey, the rewards are amazing.

<u>Preface</u>

The poetic thoughts of Fred D. Warren are on display. His words are meant to prompt thought and reflection, lyrical verse to inspire both **Ladies and Gentlemen**, intended to generate internal dialogue, and give the reader a unique perspective on the author. Rhyme flows from his mouth, exits his lips, and arrives on the pages. Enjoy and look forward to the next poetically designed literary project.

About the Author

Fred D. Warren, an aspiring poet, writes best when stressed, facing difficult challenges in LIFE. He's a son and father, residing in Kansas City, Missouri.

__Desire__

Her diamonds are rare, very hard to find
but dominant once the perfect king transcends.
I massaged her intellect and balanced her emotions
as I explored her continent and the countries within.

Her melinated legs barley spread apart.
Her mind, body, and spirit intertwine like a puzzle.
She speaks with intellect, walks with confidence
and her character is that of a true goddess.

Her body is the natural state of existence.
She is pure, clean and kept together like Pangea.
She allows my strong, masculine hands to play the role
of plate tectonics.

My touch sends powerful vibrations flowing
Through her soul.
I enjoy kissing the stretch marks on her figure.
Her body is like thunder clinging to the black sky.

I can feel the juices flowing as I caressed her thighs.
Her soft hands gently searched my person
with lustful thirst and captured my shaft.

She gave off exotic moans as she held it
biting her lips as her panties continued to cry.
My hands resting on her breasts, I slowly lowered my head,
placing my lips on her yoni
and began to drink from the fountain of life.

My thirst is quenched and now it is time to penetrate.
Long, hard, deep strokes of wonderful discoveries

as I accelerate and reverse inside of her warm, precious ovaries.

Positive vibes as she saddles on top and ride.
The both of us connecting on deeper levels as we soul tie.
The smell of her perfume and aroma got my body overheating.

It is time to free my exotic emotions.
I can feel it, as she climaxes multiple times.
Now it is my turn to release life into her universe.

My acceleration is moving beyond the speed limit
as I thrust harder, and explored the deepest part of her body
while her honey trickled down my shaft.

The stiffness of my body along with my shaft
crashed as I exploded. Like a volcano erupting,
I planted my seeds while gripping her neck.
Both of our bodies in desperate need of rest.
After the desirous journey concluded
I lay on my back while she falls asleep on my chest.

Bamboozled

In my mind she was my friend until the end.
The queen that I had chosen.
My coffee when I awake.
My sunshine during dark moments.

In my mind she was my lover godsend.
I was full of surprises.
Her favorite summertime skirts, outdoor bonfires, roses and candle lit
dinners by the peaceful lake.
She was the pacemaker to my heart, a major component.

Like a spider's web perfectly engineered.
A trawlers patience when catching fish.
A copperhead waiting to bite.
Her manipulative maneuvers slowly flowed into my life
by element of surprise.

Her intentions started out candid but gradually disappeared.
The toxic venom kisses from her penetrated my soul without warning
not even a hiss.
Impaired appetites made it hard to feast under moonlight.

In my mind I thought eye was her only one
Blinded by love with my feelings torn A P A R T
she quickly switched gears and disposed of my heart.

The bar is calling me, and Grey Goose is my companion.
Drunk conversations with myself,
tears strolling down my face soaking my shirt
I would never heal from the hurt she caused me.
It is true my childhood friend and I was sharing the same skirt.

His End

She got manipulated misused and abused.
Her body punctured, eyes blackened, and swollen from masculine fists
resulted in her becoming a frequent emergency room guest.

He would enter our home and complain without gratitude.
The house better be clean from top to bottom,
laundry washed, clothes ironed and
she'd better have his meals warm and ready was his expectations.

While he slammed his fists into her lips
and smashed the beer glass upside her head
the child sat afraid, not knowing what to do and watched her cry.

He rapidly vacated the premises.
Blood dripping from her lips and head
slurred soft words came flowing from my mommy's mouth
"I just wanna die"
"I just wanna die"
"Lord where are you God why"

She is getting older and so is the child.
She forgave him for abusing her.
He did 6 years in prison and returned to our home.
She must really love him, and the child can't figure out why.
He must comprehend that the child is not the same scared little guy.

He had a bad temper and couldn't control it.
The hard liquor caused him to lash out with unbalanced emotions.
He grabbed her by the hair and kicked her down the basement stairs.

The child premeditated and patiently waited for this moment.
Since the age of 10 the child had vengeance on his brain.

The 38 special the child borrowed from his friend would soon put the
woman's abuser to end.

The abuser turned around and met the barrel of the gun. His
face sweating, eyes wide, and hands held towards the sky
he took a deep breath saying
"I don't wanna die"
"I don't wanna die"
"Youngblood please oh God why"

The child's face cold and heart numb.
He emptied out on his chest piercing the abuser's heart and lungs.
The child's mom panicking, screaming and yelling why.
My eyes met mommy's and I replied
"Mommy I am sorry but I'm not that same scary little guy"

8/19/13 ---- 3/25/14

You are rapidly growing up before my eyes.
I am afraid of how the world will treat you.
I think about it in solitary.
Sharp cuts ripple through my chest and I start to cry.

I marvel at the beautiful, respectful, queen you are becoming.
I laugh at your attitude, smile at your unlimited energy
and the way that you dress yourself using lady accessories.

As you evolve and get older
please understand that this Earth is unbalanced.
You will have many challenges and at times
 different levels of stress will fall on your shoulders.

Embrace the woman that you are and
love who you are.
Accept and learn from the mistakes you are going to make
and be cautious of the companions you partake.

Always keep Allah on your mind.
Show gratitude at your highest and lowest moments.
Understand that after every struggle there is a moment of ease.

Keep a balance between excitement and sadness.
Always expect the unexpected
and remember that daddy will forever love you beyond eons.

Peace

Your soft words brought peace to my soul.
The way you hugged and kissed me brought tranquility to my soul.
You uncovered the king that was buried within me.
You are blessed with the kind of peace that can calm a million beasts.
Like instrumentals, the harmony you freely gave allowed my heart to
dance to your beat.

Like a flower, you watered and cared for me.
Your smile is like the bright sun that will never burn out.
Instead, it will always glow.
Your presence walked into my life, molded me into becoming a better
man, was much needed, and allowed me to grow.

Interdependent

Your body is precious like pearls and diamonds
a gem that should be treasured and protected
by masculine hands.

Heaven is something we should yarn.
Paradise will always rest at a woman's feet because
without her the masculine king would be incomplete.

Interdependent is how The Most High created us to live.
The very first human was lonely So, the Most High
created Eve and gave her part of Adam's rib.

Bees collect nectar and pollen to make honey.
Plants make their own food using photosynthesis.
Everything in nature is interdependent.

Human beings are created from Earth's clay
and are a part of nature.
The male and female complete each other.

The Lord of the universe is perfect
and make no mistakes.
The male and female combine and intertwine.
It is simple, the King and Queen need each other!

<u>Finally</u>

You should feel how soft and comfortable
these pillows are.
I am finally able to rest and vibe with a sky full of stars.

Now it is time for me to rest.
The chaos is gone and so is the stress.
The journey that awaits ahead is the true test.

The plotters field is filled with wasted knowledge.
Doctors, lawyers, musicians, and innovators.
Nothing but neglected talents.
I did not maximize my genius and am upset!

I am experiencing a different consciousness.
I hear the voices of those who surround me.
Screams and cries is all I hear!

Family and friends, I will always love you
but now it is time to say your final goodbye.
Don't cry, wipe those tears from your beautiful eyes.

I didn't choose to be cremated.
I couldn't see myself going out as ashes.
Instead, I chose to perish into mother Earth.

Grave diggers it is time. Please
lower me into my final resting place.
Family and friends remember this is not the end,
nor is it a goodbye.
Don't cry wipe those tears from your
beautiful eyes.

<u>Reminder!</u>

I glanced at my watch the time read 7:11
I gravitated towards the pack of skittles
that will satisfy any 17-year-old taste buds
and make them feel as if they are in heaven.

I didn't make it to my destination.
I did not make it home.
Zimmerman killed me because of the color of my skin
and left my spirit to roam.

Made of 100 percent cotton
A perfect fit for those who stand about
5'7 with long arms I am the black hoodie
that kept Travon Martin warm.

Reminder 2

They fractured my wrist and slammed me
to the ground.
That cop felt good forcing his strength to
impair and manhandle a woman.

I told him I had epilepsy
but my words fell on def ears.
I was being detained for a traffic ticket!
I was afraid!
No human came to my aid!

They killed me in my cell and
made it look like a suicide.
The system is beyond corrupt!
This bias organization is out of hand!

I cry, I cry, please help
I am Sondra Bland.

<u>Am I</u>

Am I crazy for communicating with myself?
Am I insane for answering my own questions?
People stand around perimeters passing judgements,
what am I to do?

They claim it is for my protection
while forcing me into a strait jacket,
locking me into a mental facility at an undisclosed location
because I refuse to be the puppet
that is being controlled by strings of fear.

Am I weird for not letting society control
my thinking?

All media outlets are fictitious.
Propaganda at its finest.
Am I deranged for discovering truth
and displaying it to the youth?

Am I just a lost cause?
Am I a threat to society?
Maybe
Maybe not!
I don't know Am I?

The day I died a million times

The day I turned my back and began
to walk away, you yelled out
"wait"
"wait"
Cuts rippled through my chest
as I held back tears.
I took a deep breath, turned around forcing
myself to smile, picked you up, and
walked back to the car.

I strapped you in the car seat and you
said
"now daddy kiss mommy"
"mommy kiss daddy"
Both mommy and daddy looked
at each other and said

"daddy and mommy can't do that anymore"

As the tears anxiously waited to spill from my eyes
I kissed your forehead and told you goodbye.
I got into my car and let the tears
run its course.

That was one of the biggest pills that I
had to swallow, because my soul had
died a million times.

<u>Feminist</u>

Even if he was The Most High
and gave you three Earths,
you would still label him the bad guy,
point the finger, and call him a devil
simply because he is a man.

All your life you have known men
to misuse and abuse you,
and that they are the biggest hypocrites
in your eyes.

Sister that is not his fault
Be cautious and choose wisely next time!

<u>Reality</u>

They put me in a strait jacket and forced me
to sit in a chair with my ankles shackled to its legs.

The psychiatrist showed me picture after picture
asking me to interpret their meanings to her.

First, she showed me a picture of my daughter
I said love.

Second, she showed me a picture of a deceased flower
I said life.

Third, she showed me a picture of a clock
I said patience.

Fourth, she showed me a picture of myself
I said torn.

Lastly, she showed me a picture of my ex.
I laughed and said that is the anaconda I didn't
see coming.

Full Circle

They humiliated, teased, and made fun of
me as an adolescent.

Look at the Most High Showing out.
I sat and observed as he allowed the tables to turn.

There is no need to look back
as I disregard my rearview.

The tables made a final turn.
I am older now.

Those peasants will never be able to walk this bridge again.
They were the ones who purchased the gasoline, sparked
the flame within my soul that gave me the desire,
and ambition to accomplish my goals!

<u>Tunes</u>

We both enjoyed gazing far into the stars
while having deep conversations.
She caused my soul to astral travel
inviting me into her galaxy,
wanting me to delve into her constellation.

My kisses caused her to nearly faint.
Her jet-black hair, bronze eyes
and cinnamon skin was the perfect blend.
I suckled her breast as she began to finger paint.

Her legs squirmed into fickle positions
as I continued to siphon her nipples.
A soldier for love, I was in an erogenous zone.
Her desirous yearnings commanded me to never
abandon my post until I completed the mission.

I utilized my tongue to massage and sketch
the alphabets on her clitoris.
Like a serpent swaddling its prey
she wrapped her legs around my waist.

Lustfully fighting for position,
the soft melody tunes filled the room
while her favorite artist Aaliyah sang
with ambition.
We changed positions as I rocked her boat
deep into the night and worked the middle with
aggressive, deep strokes.

<u>Memories</u>

Your love reminded me of the yearly seasons

Your dark side (Fall)

Your warm energetic outbursts (Spring)

Your wild unrehearsed straightforwardness (Summer)

Your anxiety and depression (Winter)

All of which was an odor that was impossible to eliminate.

<u>DeadBeat</u>

The deadbeat man's cry falls on deaf ears.
Untold stories and fabricated lies are often spoken from dark souls of disappointed, hurt, and resentful women.

The deadbeat is silently drowning in his own tears. He secretly relies on prayer, and constantly asks the creator to allow his depression to disappear.

Why must the deadbeat jump through loopholes just to see, care, and love his seed?
His good deeds are always overlooked, and purposely ignored.

His efforts are shunned, assassinated and deliberately washed away.
To the deadbeat's dismay, his family is constantly stressing the fact that he should just walk away.

Walk away from the hurt that is causing him harm mentally, physically, and emotionally.
Walk away from his child being caught in a tug of war battle that seems as if it will never end.

But the deadbeat refuses to throw in the towel.
Like a case being handled through the courts, he will not plead guilty instead, he will take it to trial.
He enjoys running extra miles, going above and beyond combative circumstances to remain active in his child's life.
The deadbeat will stand tall full of stamina, even if fatigue starts to settle, he will not give up

Over his child, the deadbeat will place his life on the line.

Kill or be killed, run, walk, or crawl, from the moment his child was conceived by its mother, the deadbeat made a promise to help raise, love, teach, and provide for his child.

Against all odds and crucial circumstances, the deadbeat will not ever give up on his child and throw in the towel because he is in it for the long haul.

Fellas it is simple
Stop complaining about not being able to see your child. Do what I did, set your pride behind you, take the child's mom to court and get involved in your child's life.

<u>Guilty</u>

I walked into your life while you were in the process of rebuilding yourself.
I knew that you wanted someone to uplift your spirit and I took full advantage of your vulnerability.

I was guilty of failing to lead as a man should.
I was guilty of manipulating your mind.
I was guilty of walking into your life only to accommodate my needs and leaving your heart in shambles.

I was the criminal that ruined your life, assassinated your trust, and ignored your tears.
The Most High is and will always be the one and only true judge.

If I was to stand trial for misleading you, he would appoint you as the prosecutor.
I wouldn't fully blame you for prosecuting me with maximum punishment because I deserve it.

I speak from deep within my soul and from the roots of my heart.
I apologize because I was guilty of breaking your heart.

<u>FREDISM #1</u>

He will always recollect and cherish the moments
Your character showed him how a king was supposed to be treated
More than the times you called him one.

Action speaks volumes

Truth be Told

I miss your soft touch
I miss hugging you
I miss the smell of your fragrance
I miss falling asleep with you
I miss waking up next to you
I miss your cooking
I miss your smile
I miss kissing your soft lips
I miss praying with you
I miss you teaching me
I miss leading you as a king should
I miss our conversations

As quiet as it is kept, I am still in love with you.
Do you miss me?
Are you still in love with me?

Even though we split apart,
I still haven't gotten over you.
It is a feeling I cannot let go.

When you are laying on his chest, do you still think about me?
It's crazy because while I lay next to her, I still think about and miss you.

We often find ourselves thinking that the grass is greener on the other side. We forget to take some time to heal ourselves from past heartbreaks and relationships. Learn how to heal "YOU" before jumping into another relationship. If not, you will end up like me. I have two beautiful kids by two different Queens all because I did not take the time to heal myself from the first heartbreak.

Different

He will never introduce you to his mom or grandma if you openly display your diamonds amongst the world.

He will not even consider asking your father for your hand in marriage if all he see if half nude pictures of your body.

You will not gain his love by displaying filters that dilutes your nature state, desperately begging for attention, wanting to be recognized by emojis and likes!

He is very secretive when it comes to his personal life and he doesn't need Facebook, Snapchat, Instagram, or any other social media outlet to validate his love for you.

Purest of them all

You don't have to be a barbie or model to be considered beautiful.
You are the purest of them all.
You are admirable, classy, and charming in your natural state.
Photoshopped pictures, altered faces, followed by a flock of likes and emojis, dilutes your natural existence!
It is ok to be YOU, all WOMAN, no modifications. Just simply pure and NATURAL.

<u>YOU</u>

What about the times she gave YOU her undivided attention?
Remember when she loved YOU more than you loved yourself?

What about the times she forgave YOU for stepping out on her with
other women?
Remember when she gave YOU her full trust even when you gave her
every reason in the universe not to?

What about the times she ignored your flaws?
Remember when she gave YOU strong, pure, compassionate, and
unconditional love?

What about the lies YOU constantly told her just to mute her cries?
Remember when she finally had enough?
Remember when she found the strength to move on?

Do YOU remember?
Oh… you want to cherish her now?
The fingers are pointing directly towards YOU

YOU had your chance, this chapter is final
It is too late because she is no longer around.

I Still Wonder Why

I don't think I can ever forgive you
for what you did to me!

We were young
still in our teens.

Were you scared?
Why did you make that treacherous decision?
Did you really love me?

If so, why did you make the final verdict
behind my back?

The choice you made shot arrows through my flesh and penetrated my
soul.

J.M.W. abortion was never supposed to be part of the plan. Even though
it's been a decade, I still think about what you did and at times wonder
what our child could have been.

I Will Never Forget

You took so many losses
but recognized your weaknesses and overcame the minor
setbacks you encountered.

Your favorite color was blue,
and you had a passion for fast
cars.

You had the hustle game in a guillotine
along with the fruits that bore your labor.

Jealous and envious companions placed
themselves in your cypher,
but you saw the good within people, and
overlooked their serpent characteristics.

I will never feel comfortable, nor will I
ever look at a beauty salon, or barbershop
with a soothing relaxation feeling again.

Your grind was on steroids and the
envious couldn't stomach it.
You will forever be in my mind.
I will forever love you C.J.B
Peace Extreme Love and Respect

Disgusted Pt. 1

Sometimes I look at you with disgust!
The fire in my eyes erupts when I
think about your infidelity.
You played a major role in my distrust.

You introduced me to your male companion.
We greeted each other as kings and embraced each other with warm
smiles but I had no idea that the two of you were intertwining and
romancing.

He was a guest at our wedding which should have been a blessing.
Instead, your serpent desires came to light when I caught both you and
him performing fallacious activities on our bedspread.

You betrayed my love!
You shattered my trust!
Sometimes I look at you with disgust!1!

To be continued.

<u>To the beautiful women</u>

Just to be in your presence is a blessing.
Just to be able to sit at the dinner table with you is a blessing.

To open car doors for you is a blessing.
Being able to provide for you is an honor.
To have the strength to protect you is a blessing.

Being able to pray next to you is a blessing.
Being able to greet you when you come home is a blessing.
Being able to hug, kiss, and smell your fragrance is an honor.
Being able to buy you diamonds and roses is a blessing.

What you give me I cannot ever replace in a lifetime. It is my duty to
pay you back for the one thing I can't do and that is to bring a child into
this world. Paradise will always rest at your feet.

Can We Teach Each Other?

She needed her thirst quenched, mind stimulated and asked how I can go about accomplishing those things.

I sat her down, looked deep into her eyes and said
Will you be open to letting me caress your mind for intelligence?
Will you allow me to speak to your soul with verbification and action?
Will you allow me to massage my intellect on your subconscious?

Do you understand that you are special?
Do you comprehend that you are powerful?
Do you realize that you can make an impaired man strong?
Do you understand that you can make a vigorous, masculine man stronger?
Can I make love to you spiritually and mentally?
Can I cause your panties to cry without sexual penetration?
Will you learn with me?
Can I teach you about the world from a different angle?

Do you have an open mind?
Can we teach each other?

Encourage

I encourage you to read
I encourage you to remain focused
I encourage you to never give up
I encourage you to smile
I encourage you to remain humble
I encourage you to create
I encourage you to elevate
I encourage you to enjoy the process
I encourage you to motivate
I encourage you to love
I encourage you to love yourself
I encourage you to forgive
I encourage you to believe in yourself
I encourage you to ignore the naysayers
I encourage you to be consistent
and most importantly
I encourage you to constantly do a self-evaluation and always keep The
Most High on your mind.

Forever Embedded

The day that I stabbed my teacher
you gave up on me.
I was a problem child.
It was six of us.
You raised us as best as you could and did a wonderful job!
You placed me in western Missouri.
That is when my grand mommy stepped
in.

She taught me how to read, write, pray, count money, and how to love
myself.

Momma I still love, cherish, and honor you.
I don't hold you accountable for the choices you made.
I was out of control and needed help.

Grand mommy,
Thank you for taking me in when the world gave up on me.
You should me unconditional love.
You put your life on pause to help me with mines.
I am so thankful and forever embedded in your debt.
Love you eons grand mommy.

<u>Reminder For Elevation</u>

Pain hurts and it leaves permanent scars.
Pain is something you slowly learn to accept.
I don't think you can ever forget the pain someone has caused you.

To forgive and forget is a fictitious statement!

In order to move forward with your life, you must learn how to forgive.
Forgive the person who caused you harm
not for their comfort, but for your sanity and peace of mind.

Backbone

You are the architect of my imagination,
the sun that warms my spirit
listen for the sound
can you hear it?

It's my heart beating with excitement to the vibration of your soft,
charming, sweet voice.
You keep the king within me well balanced.
You are the pillars of my life and the foundation that aids my creativity.

(It really is a man's world
but without a woman… a man will always be incomplete)

Black

Black is love
Black is beyond beautiful
Black is the source of peace
Black is amazing
Black is kindness
Black is universal
Black is powerful
Black is king
Black is queen
Black is classy
Black is masculine
Black is feminine
Black is energy
Black is innovative
Black is original
Black is the provider
Black is the protector
Black is the teacher
Black!
Black!
Black!
It really is a blessing to be black!

Respect other individuals no matter the color of their skin! Let us love, honor, embrace and respect each other as human beings! Simply Simple

<u>Intoxicated Love</u>

Your love is poison like Hennessey
satisfying my temporary desire, and
quenching my thirst while I accept the harm you are causing me.

You only love me when Hennessey controls your spirit,
but once your body sobers and mind is no longer impaired,
you get excited when I am at my lowest.

One minute you hate me
and within the next hour you love me.

Your love is like Hennessey
poison to my mind, body, and wellbeing,
only satisfying my temporary desires,
quenching my thirst while I constantly accept
the harm you are causing me.

What If

What if you could admire me like the mirror you stand in front of?
What if you could love me the same way you adore your followers on social media?

What if you could thirst for my attention the same way you rush to social media and take selfies?

What if I can bring out the real beauty within you minus the altered photoshopped pictures?

What if I can be your open diary?
I will listen to you express your feelings without being judgmental.
You wouldn't have to vent to strangers on social media.

What if I want to build and teach our family without structuring our relationship off a celebrity?

What if's can be possibilities
It is simply up to you.

<u>Solitary</u>

Navigate me to a room
close all curtains
lock all doors
and turn off the lights.

There is no one to communicate with.
I am alone.
Its peaceful.
Just how I expected it would be.

I need some time to think.
Just a few months of isolation.
They protest that I change my introvert ways
but quietness and tranquility are beneficial for the soul.

My energy is slowly drifting, and its urgent that I balance them.
Meditation is key.
The way I think is critical.

Please navigate me to a room
close all curtains
lock all doors
turn off every light
AND LEAVE ME FUCK ALONE!

Real Men

Dear King

It is ok to cry.
It is ok to feel depressed.
It is ok to tell your children that you love them.
It is ok to treat your queen like a goddess.
It is ok to buy her roses.
It is ok to open car doors for your Queen.
It is ok to be a kid at heart.
It is ok to express your emotions.

King!!!
Don't let society suppress your feelings!
Don't let society tell you that real men don't cry!

Society teaches us that crying is for weak men
but that is not true.
Crying releases stress, heal and allows us to move forward in life

King,
Just remember after you finish crying
gather up the fragments and move on.

Mentally Gone

Our relationship ended years
before we finally called it quits.

Mentally I had given up.
I tried to teach, lead, and uplift your
spirits.

I saw potential within you.
I loved you more than you loved
yourself and that was my downfall.

Over the years I finally realized what
my grandma meant when she said
"you can't change anybody but yourself"

I had to let the relationship go
and set myself free.

I loved and cared about you too much.
I just wished that you had given me
the same energy when it came to you loving me.

Enjoy The Ride

Please let time heal your troubles.
Let patience bandage your injured wounds
caused by life's trials and tribulations.

Allow balance to take control of your emotions.
Allow the power of forgiveness the ability
to flow into your heart.

Let the influence of giving
spark a desire of hope for those
who are less fortunate.

Do not place time limits on your journey.
Learn to accept the challenges that arise
and enjoy the road to success.

Just relax and enjoy the ride.

Patience

Learn how to communicate with her soul
when dark clouds decide to loiter above her head.
Do not expose the secrets she once shared with you to the world.

Try not to judge her based upon the load she carries.
Her past mistakes are the steppingstones towards greatness.

King be patient with your goddess.
Caress her intellect with soft, comforting, electric
words.

In return
She will cling to your guidance just as thunder
grips the sky.

<u>Feelings I never experienced</u>

Hey handsome how was work?
Did you drink enough water?
Did lunch satisfy your stomach?

Let me help you undress out of your
work clothes.
Your bath water is ready.

I know you've been on your feet
all day so I added some Epsom salt to it.

Dinner is in the oven.
It's your favorite dish
Lasagna, garlic bread, and salad.

Let me massage your body
and take the stresses you hold away.

Thank you for being more than a provider.
Thank you for being a real King.
I am very grateful to have you in my life.

Until this day I've never experienced
this kind of treatment.

<u>Solo</u>

But

When you are at your
lowest and suffering from
depression like I do
you have no choice but to constantly
fight the negative thoughts within
to stay happy.

It is important that you regularly
alter your way of thinking.

Born alone.
Die alone.

In the end,
The world is a lonely place and
nobody cares.
The only thing that is promised in this life is death and nobody gets out
alive.

<u>Blind</u>

I should have seen the warning signs.

I was reckless, took her to the finest places
where we both got lost in our childhood imaginations.

I was head over heels for this woman.
I didn't mind paying her bills.

In conclusion,
I paid the devastating price and brought
that heartbreaking experience.

Her friends laughed as I called multiple times.
It is true I got lolli popped licked
and played for a sucker!

It happens to the best of us. The only solution to this problem would be
to gather up the fragments and move on.

Independent

The more you adopt the independent syndrome
and the "I don't need a man" attitude,
he will soon lose sight and focus when it comes to being a leader,
provider, and protector.

The king will not rest his head where he is not wanted or needed.
God created man to be the providers, maintainers, and protectors of
women.

Women,
Be cautious of adopting the independent mindset!
Treating him like you don't want or need him will cause him to rapidly
find someone who believes in him and being interdependent.

<u>Reminder</u>

Ladies

He is still trying to free himself of the mental and physical stresses
society has placed on his shoulders.

Don't focus on what you can gain
instead, focus on what you can give.

Be more than his peace.
Be the medicine that cures his aches and pains.

Be the woman who takes the stress off his shoulders.
Be patient with him.

Remember he is still trying to free himself of the mental and physical
stresses society has placed on his shoulders.

Love him
Be patient with him.

<u>Transition</u>

Time healed his open wounds.

He had no choice but to gather up the fragments
and move on.
He finally got over you
and no, he didn't find someone else
instead, he found himself.

I'm sorry

Excuse me
Do I have your consent to undress you with my eyes?
I apologize, but it is a challenge for me to lower my gaze.

I praise the way you talk, walk with confidence,
and hold your head high with pride.

I did my homework, surveyed your frame, calculated and carefully
studied the latitude, and longitude along with the circumference of your
thighs.

I don't mean to sound rude or creepy
I do apologize.
Please understand that it is a challenge for me to lower my gaze and not
undress you with my eyes.

Just be patient

It is better to wait
days, months, or years for love
to willingly flow into your life than to
stay with someone who does not honor
love and respect you.

Be patient with yourself.
Allow real love to find you instead of searching for it.

You can't save everyone!

You shouldn't have to carry the world
on your shoulders and be forced to move mountains.
You shouldn't have to deal with societies stresses and the troubles it
brings

When I asked you what was wrong
you never told me.

That is why we did not work out.
You never wanted to talk about your problems
instead, you kept them bottled up inside.

You were a ticking time bomb.
You needed love and attention.

I wanted to ease your pain and comfort your soul,
but you never allowed me. All I wanted to do was be
there for you and give you what you needed without
you asking for it.

Reality kicked in and I finally realized
that I can't save everyone
not even you.

Ended before ending

I spent less than 60 seconds getting over you
and more time falling in love with you.

Our relationship ended years before we finally decided to call it quits.
Mentally I had already divorced our toxic relationship and moved on.

Toxic relationships are a waste of time and energy. Trust your instincts
and vibes. Know when to finally quit and let go.

<u>It wouldn't feel right</u>

The thought of you reentering into my
life makes me paranoid.
It makes my awareness stronger as
if it is my first time getting high.

I loved the person that you once were,
but the human that you are today
I really dislike.

If I allowed you to come back into my life
my soul wouldn't feel right letting you back in.

Just the thought of you walking into my life
makes me vomit and paranoid.
Those thoughts give me more reasons to stay
away from your serpent spirit.

Question

Why is it that society teaches us to judge a
person based upon the clothes, cars and homes
they have with their eyes instead of observing their true
character and soul?

It's easy to judge a person based upon the
materialistic things they have. Try judging a person
based upon how they treat other people and their character.
You might not like the results you come up with.

<u>Indecisive</u>

I don't want you to come back into my life
and no, I do not miss you!

I miss you, please walk back into my life.
I was angry and yes, I really do love you.

I can't stand the sight of you.
I never have and will not ever need you.
I vomit at the thought of you.

I miss seeing your face.
I need your encouraging words.
the thought of you makes me smile.

But then again
I don't want you to come back into my life and no I do not miss you!

It's true
I am indecisive, dazed and confused.

<u>Lesson understood</u>

The next time love tries to invite
herself into my life,
I will be patient, control my desires,
and make sure that she loves my soul
before I allow my body to lay next to and touch hers.

Facts

The moment I found peace
tranquility, and comfort in depression,
I had the ability to meet sadness, and fear head on.
I gathered up the shattered fragments and allowed the agony to slowly
leave my soul.

Depression is a serious matter.
If you are feeling low, and ready to quit
I beg you to look fear in the eye and defeat it.
Go to war with fear, sorrow and doubt, and watch you come out on top!

The surgeons can't fix this

I have purple hearts on my
chest and shoulders from pain that I have encountered.
I have combat wounds and scars all over my body
from promises that were never fulfilled.

Promises are made to be broken
that is why I never make them.
Never put your trust in human beings
because they will fail you every time.